NATIONAL GEOGRAPHIC

What Has Changed?

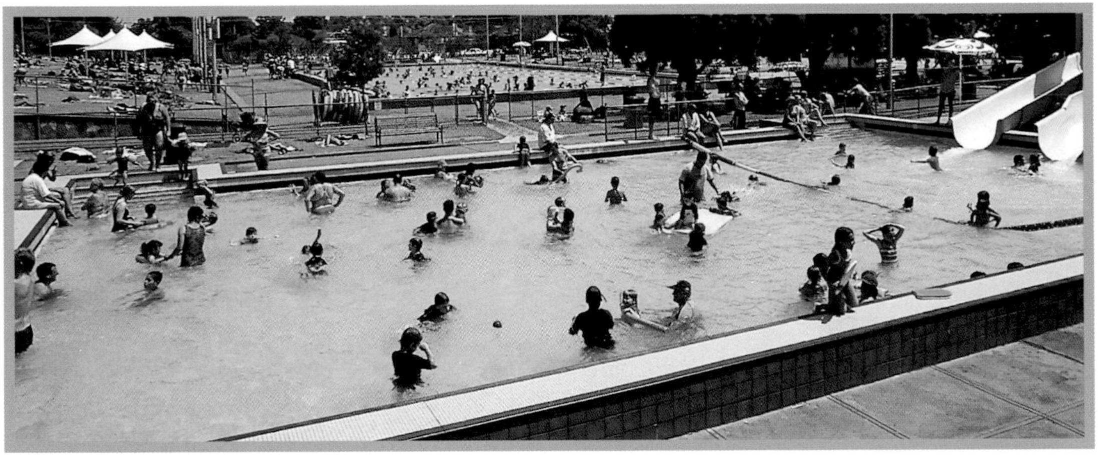

Karl Jensen

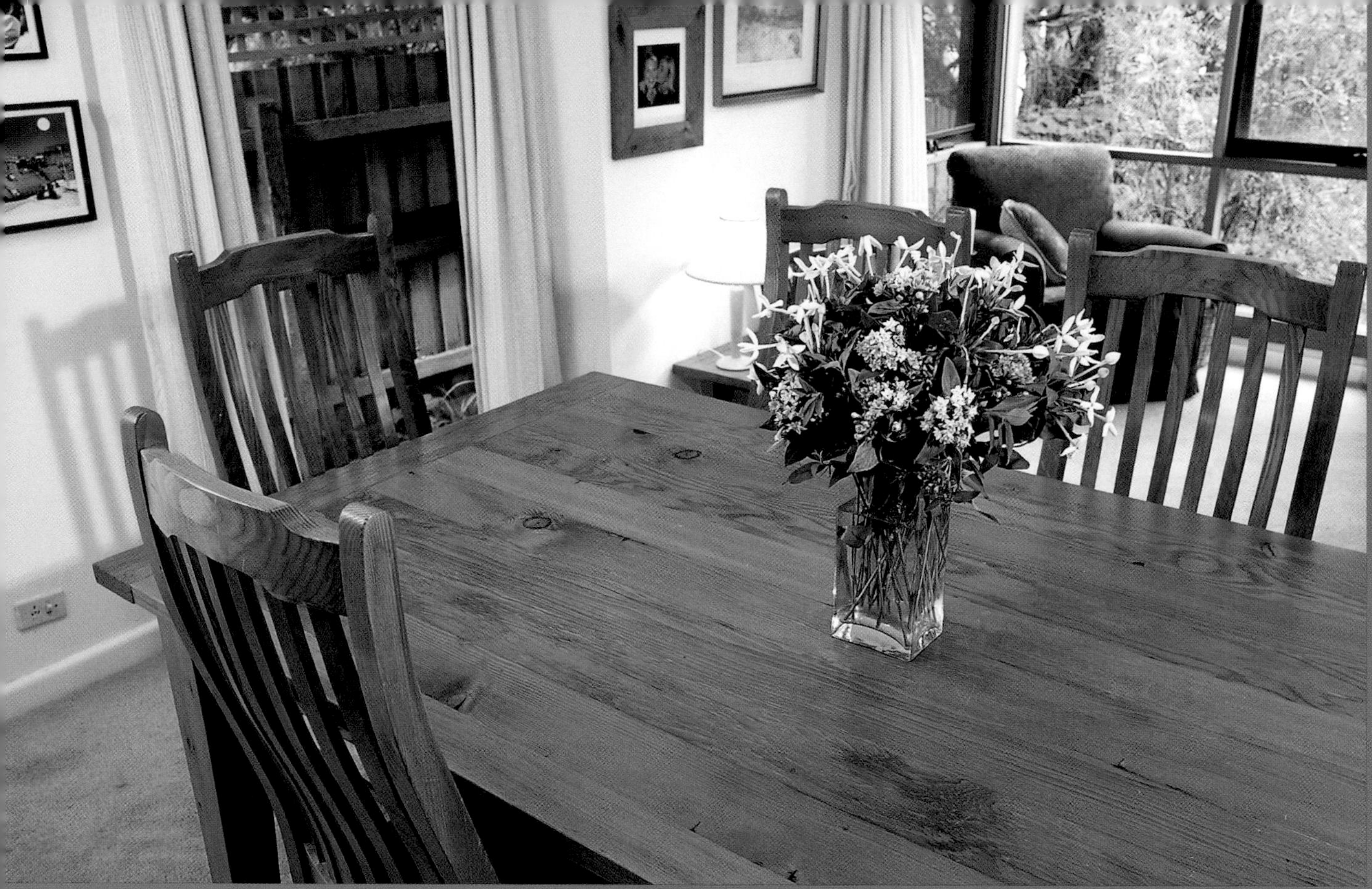

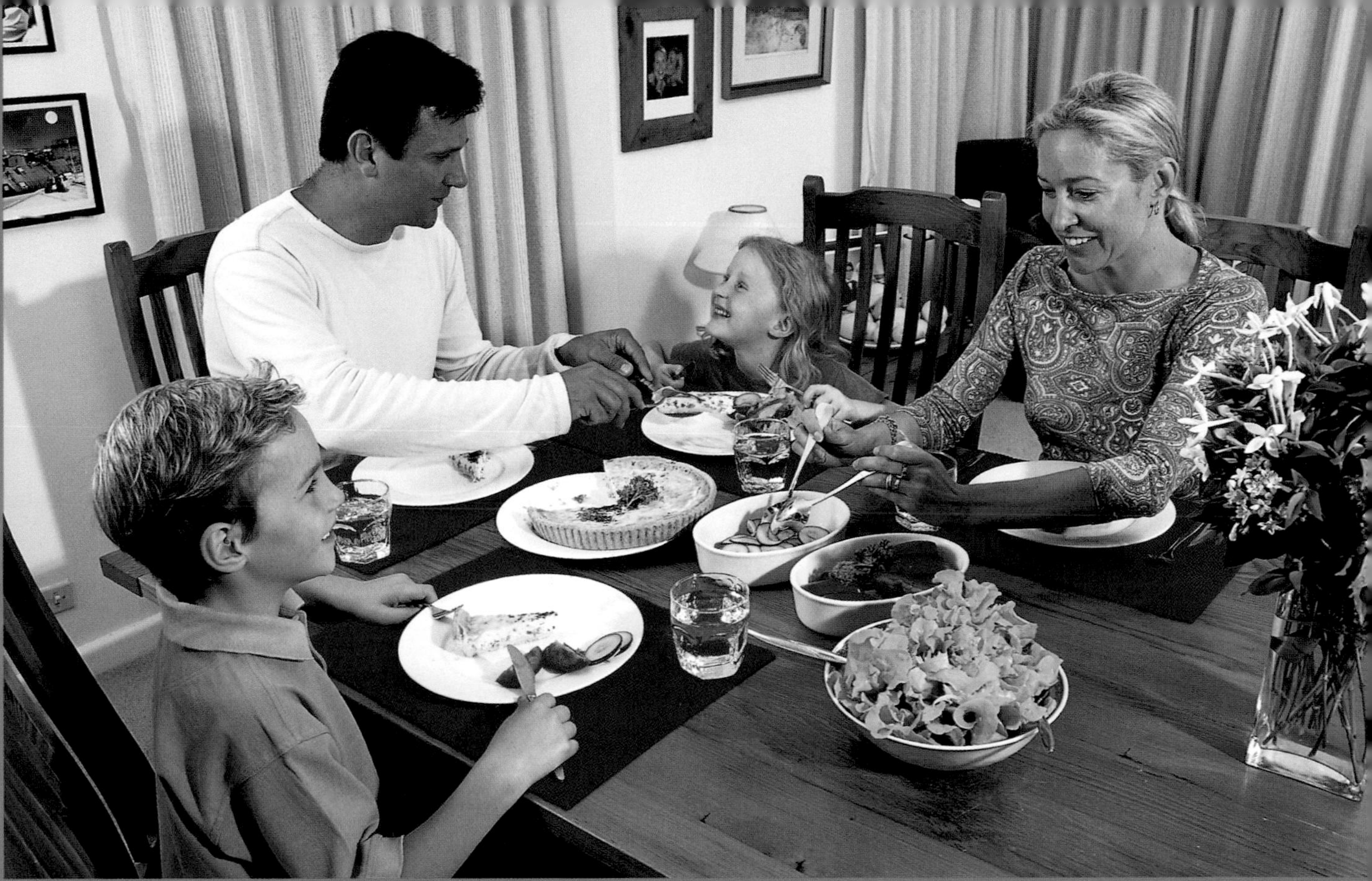

What has changed?

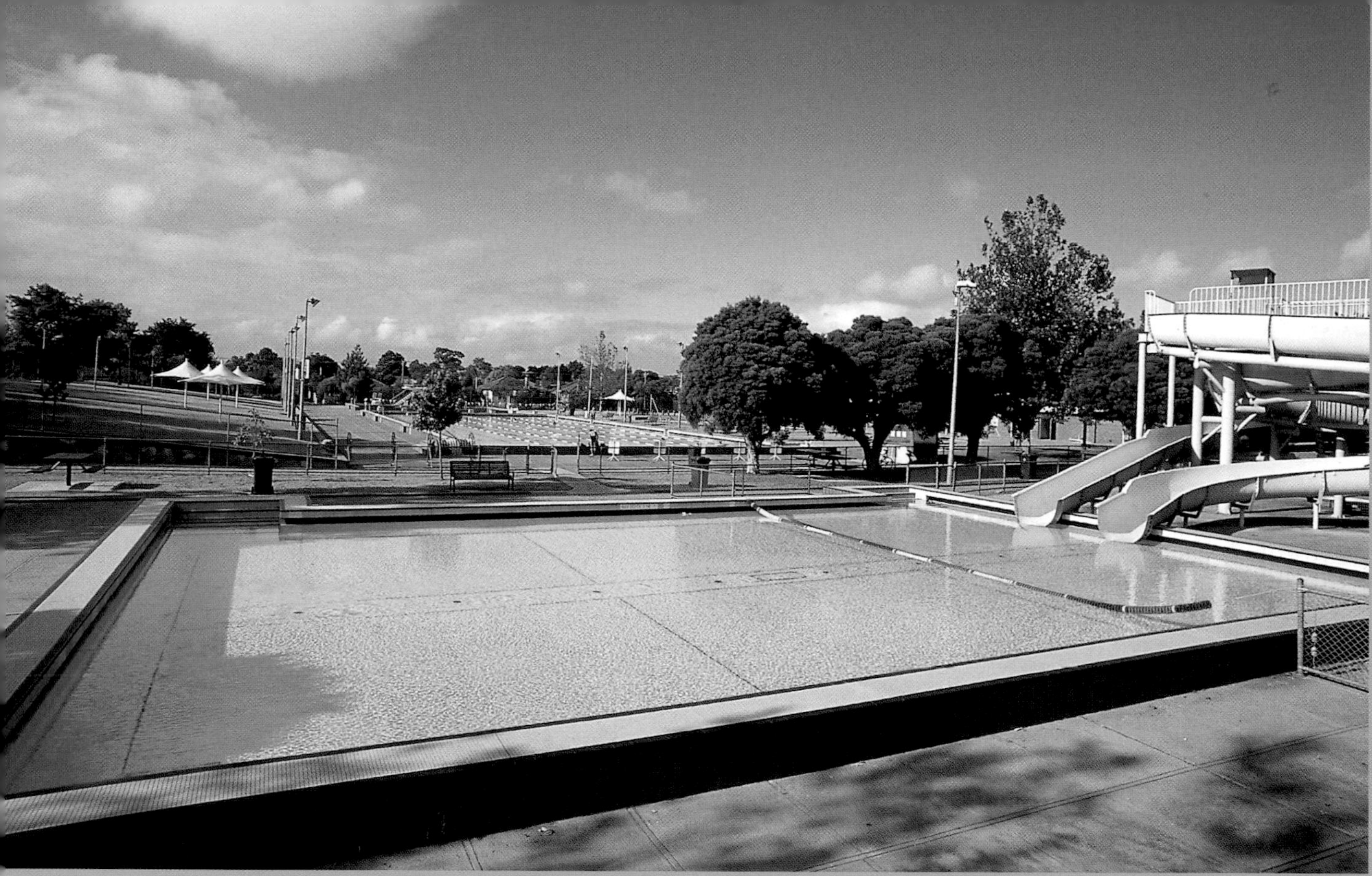

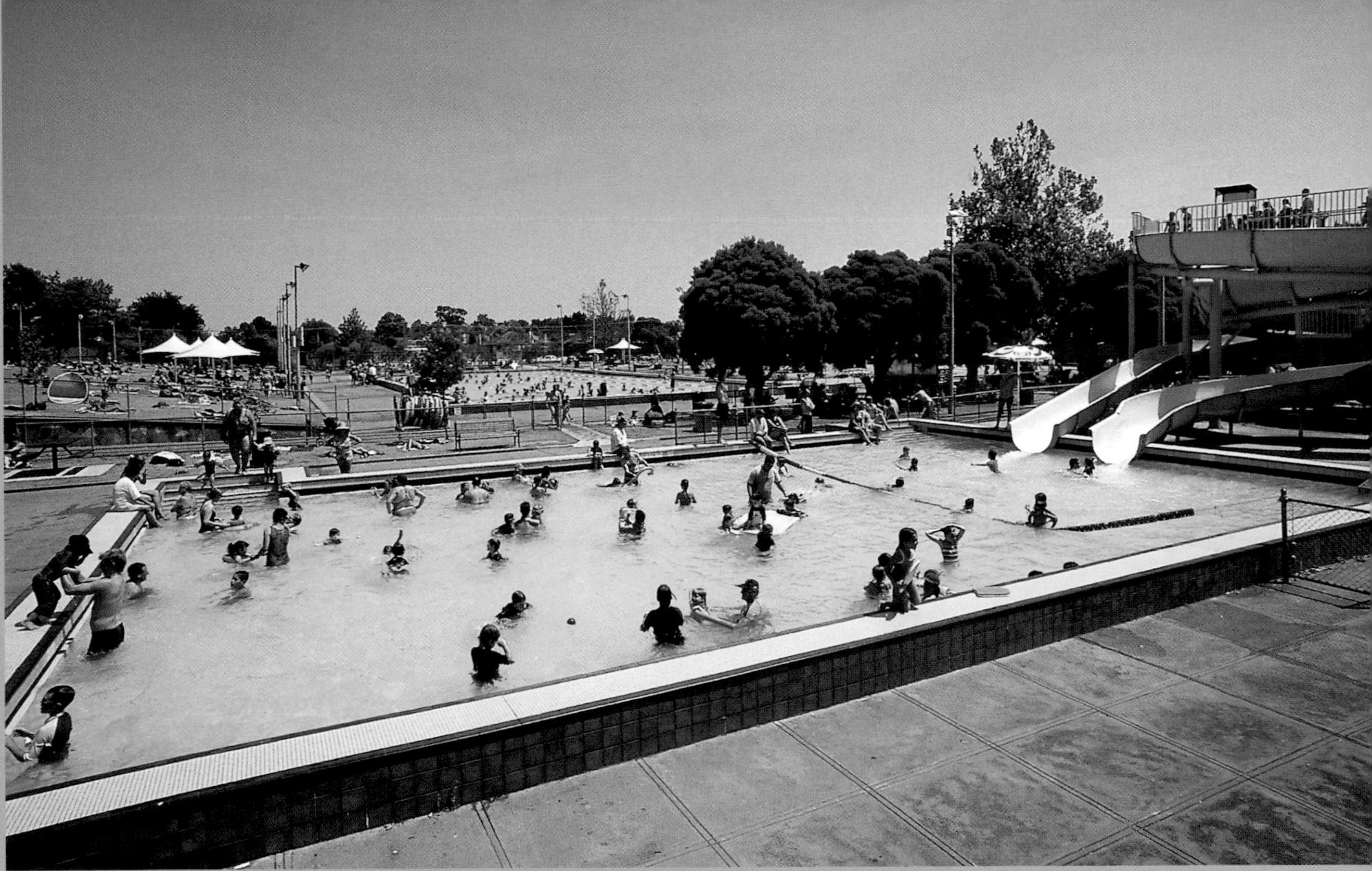

What has changed?

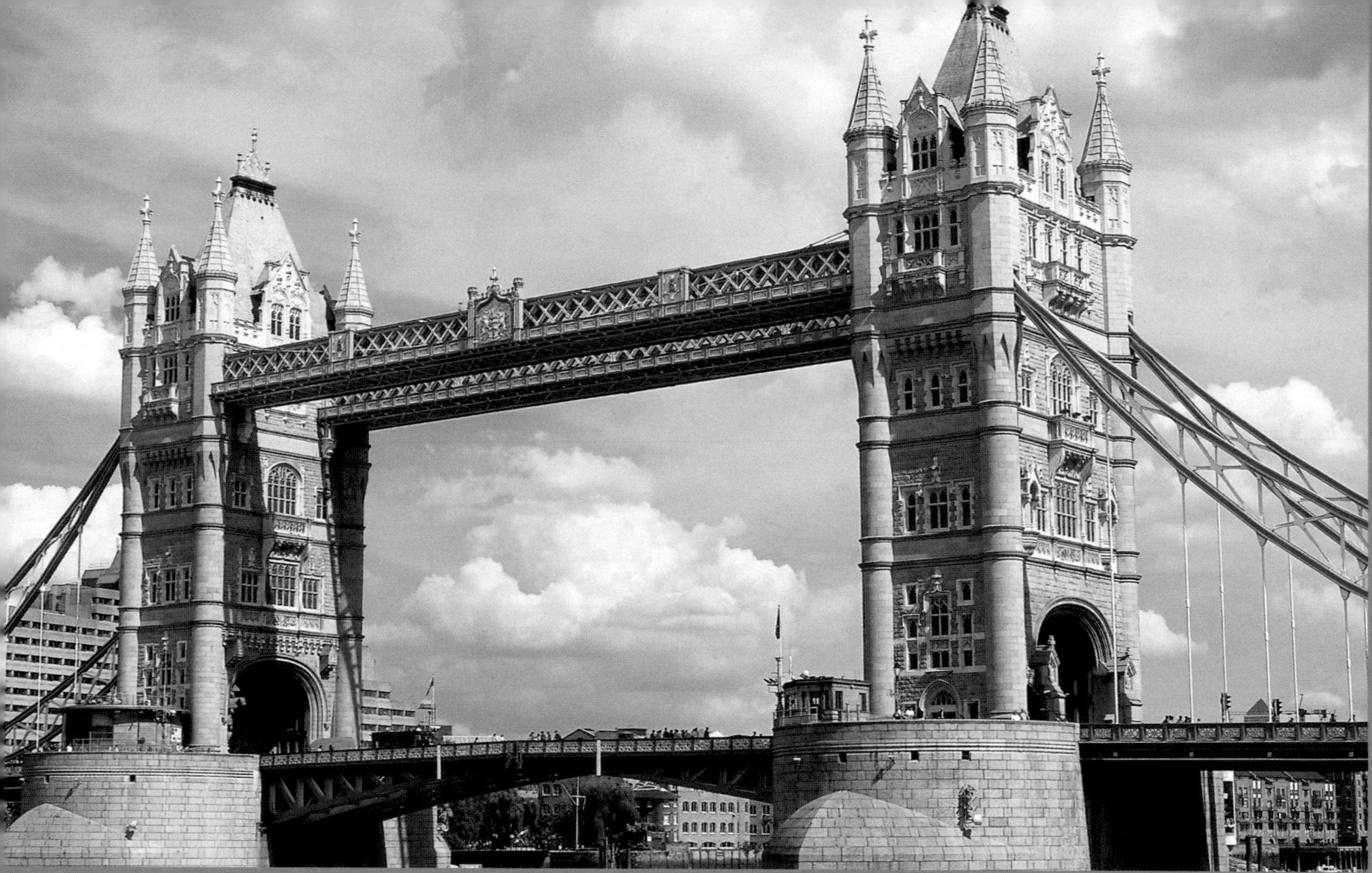

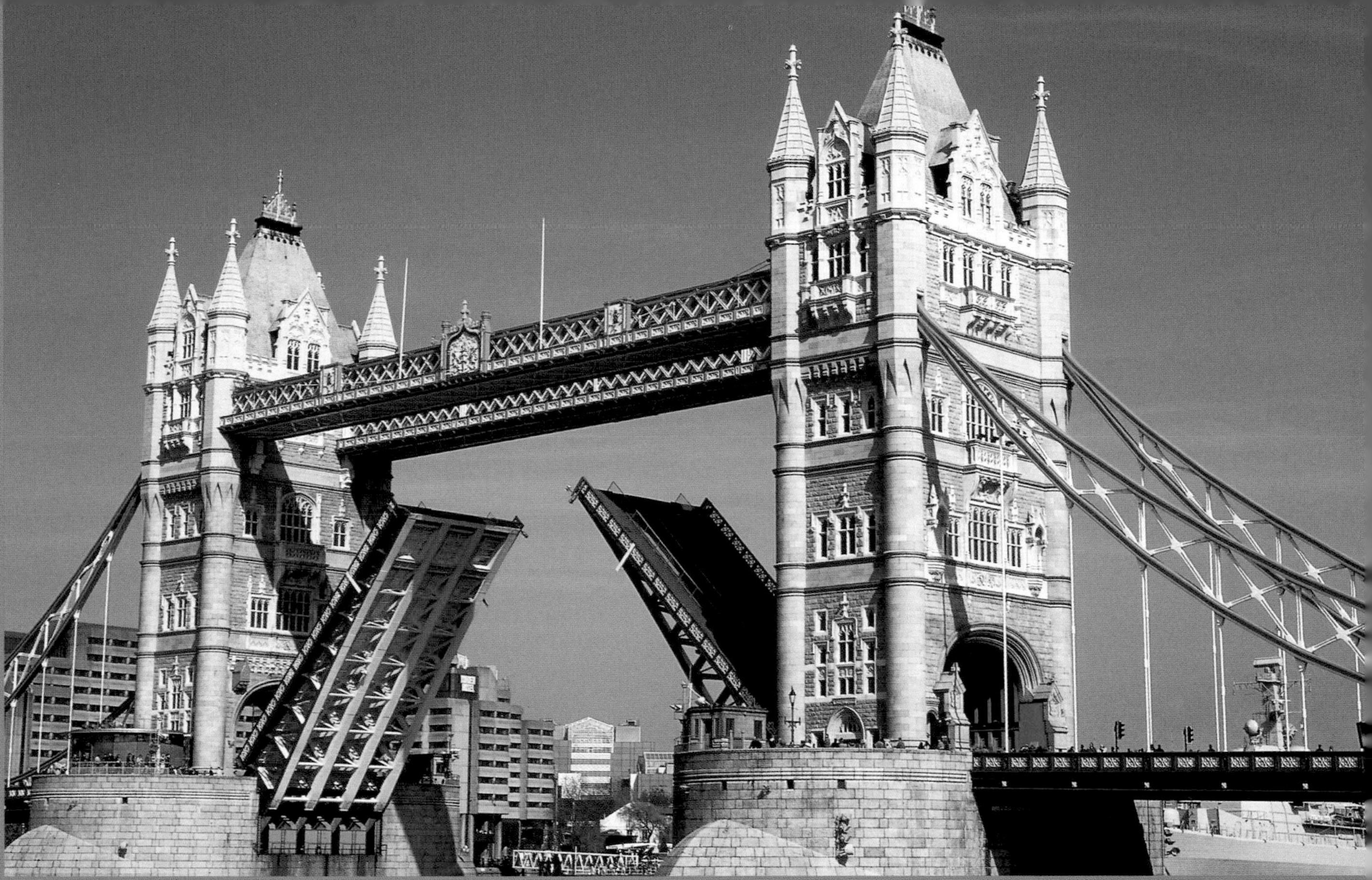

What has changed?

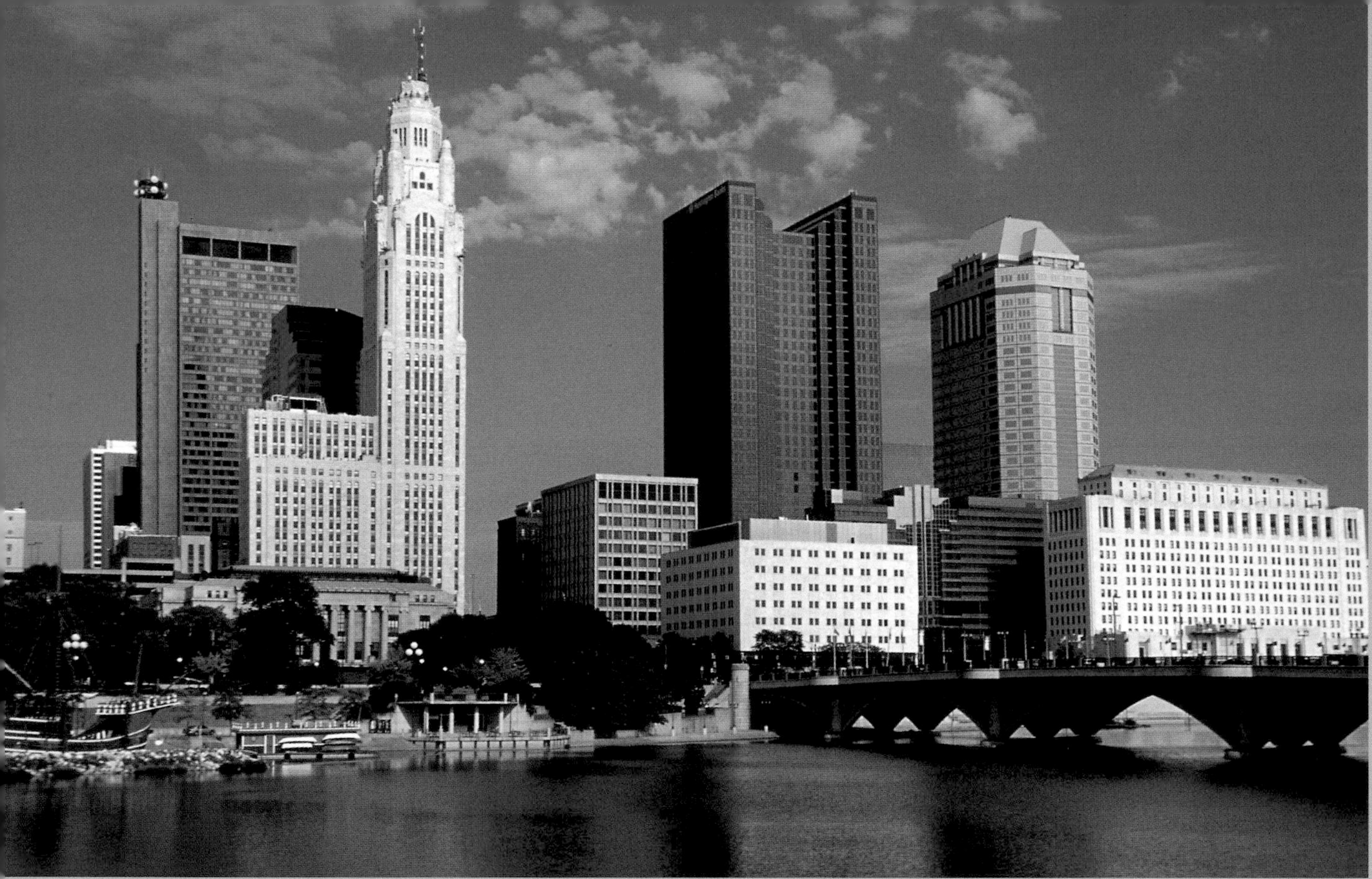

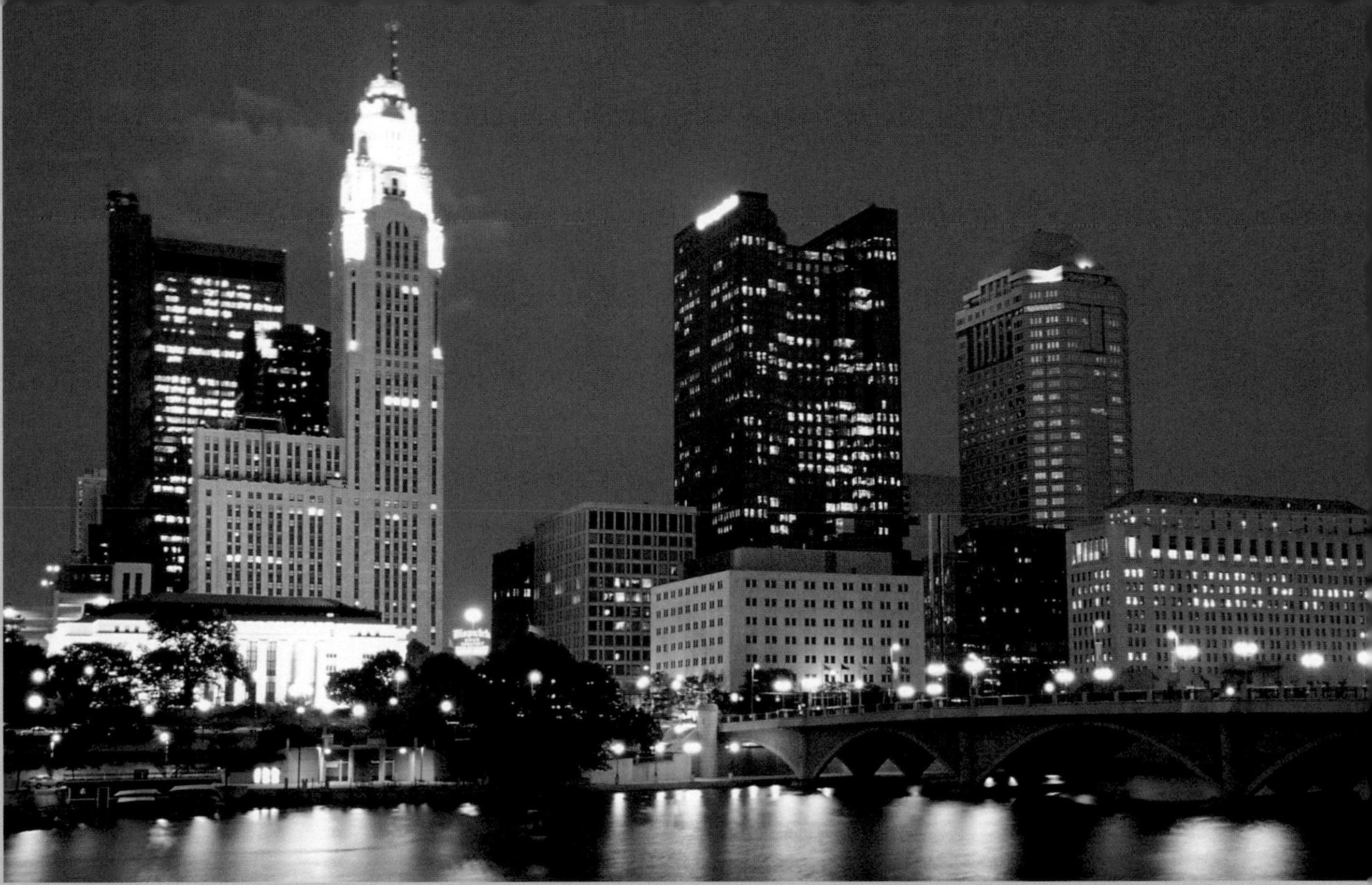

What has changed?

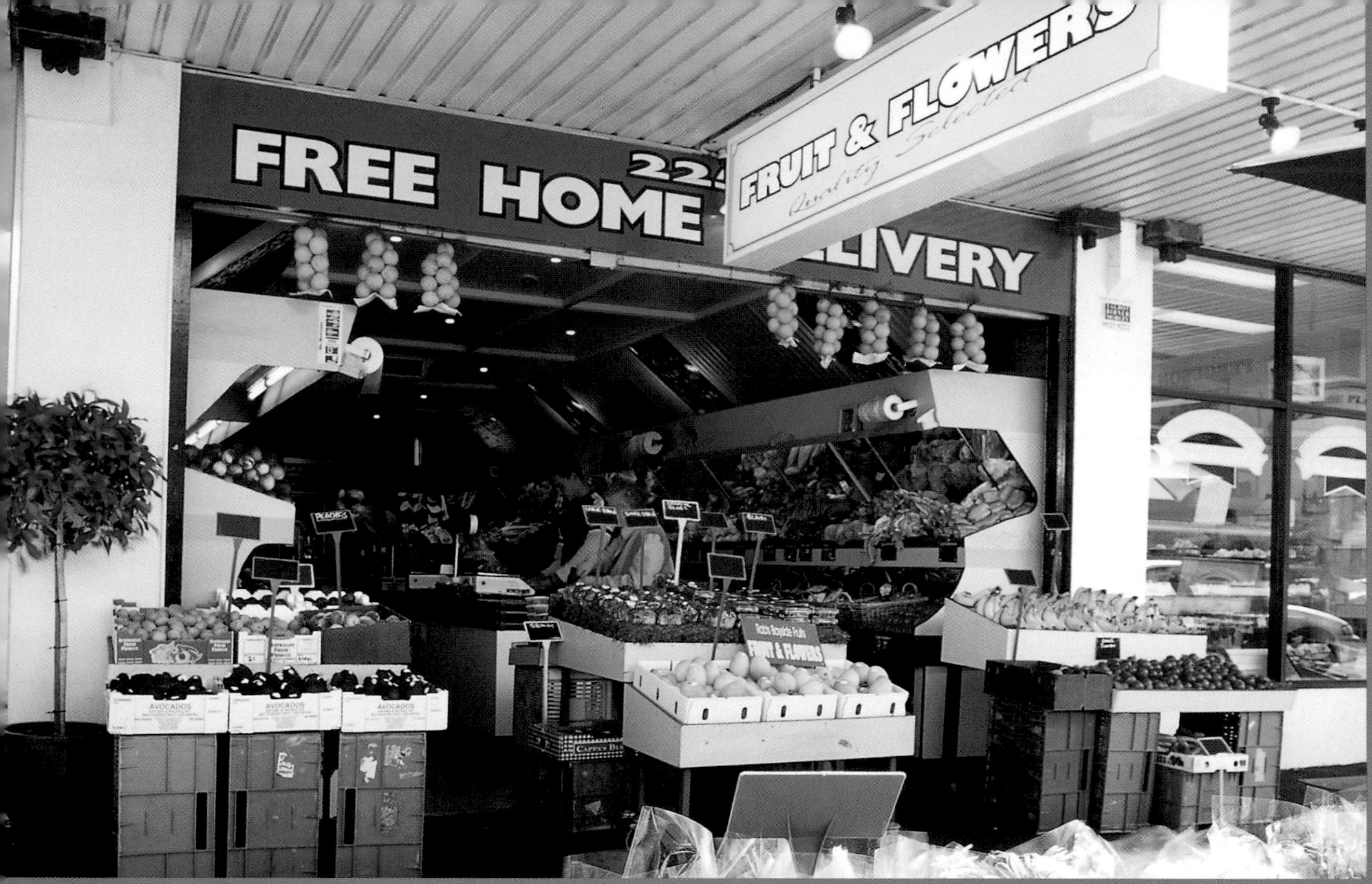

FREE HOME
DELIVERY
FRUIT & FLOWERS
Quality Selected
AVOCADOS

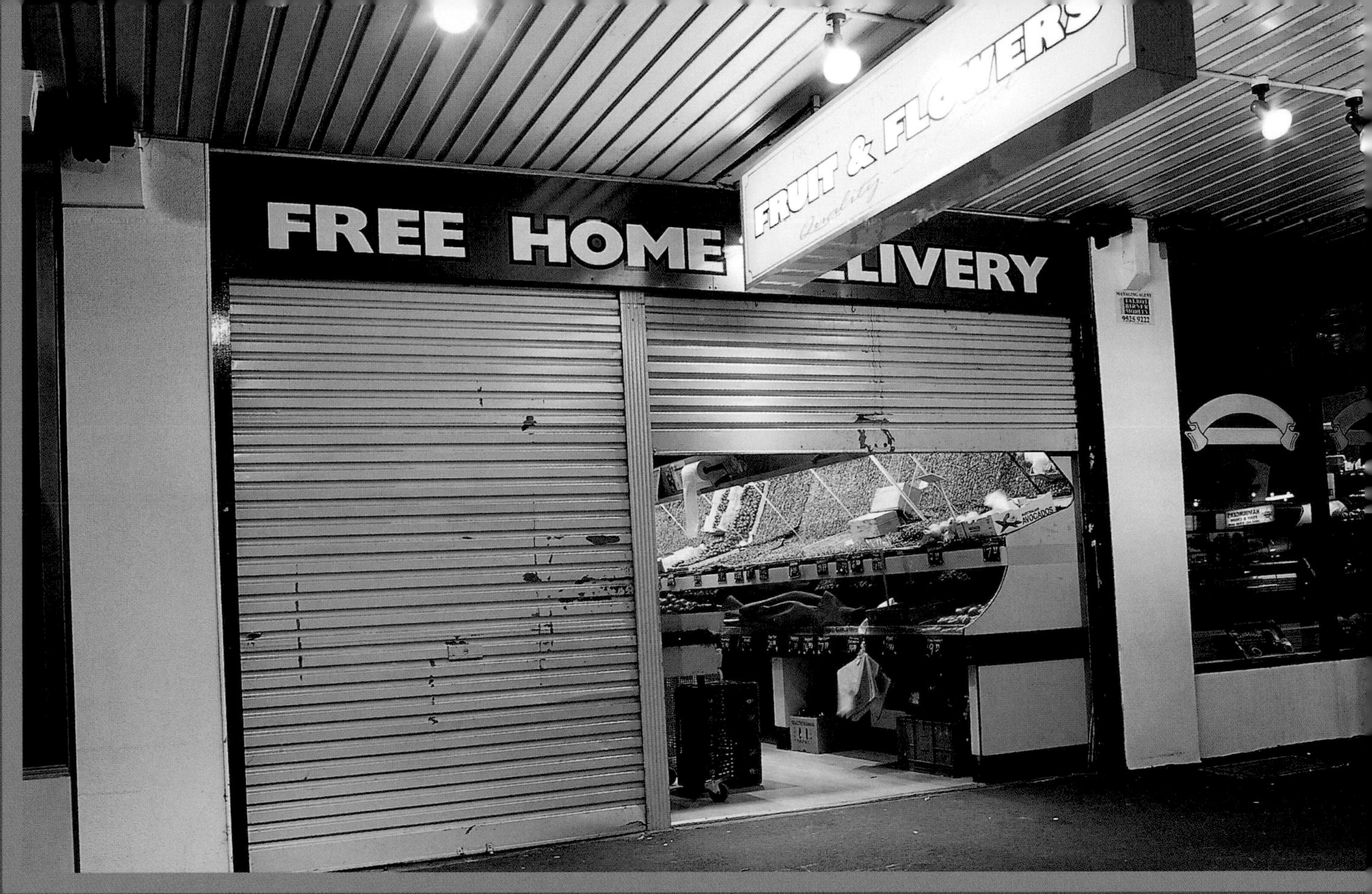

What has changed?

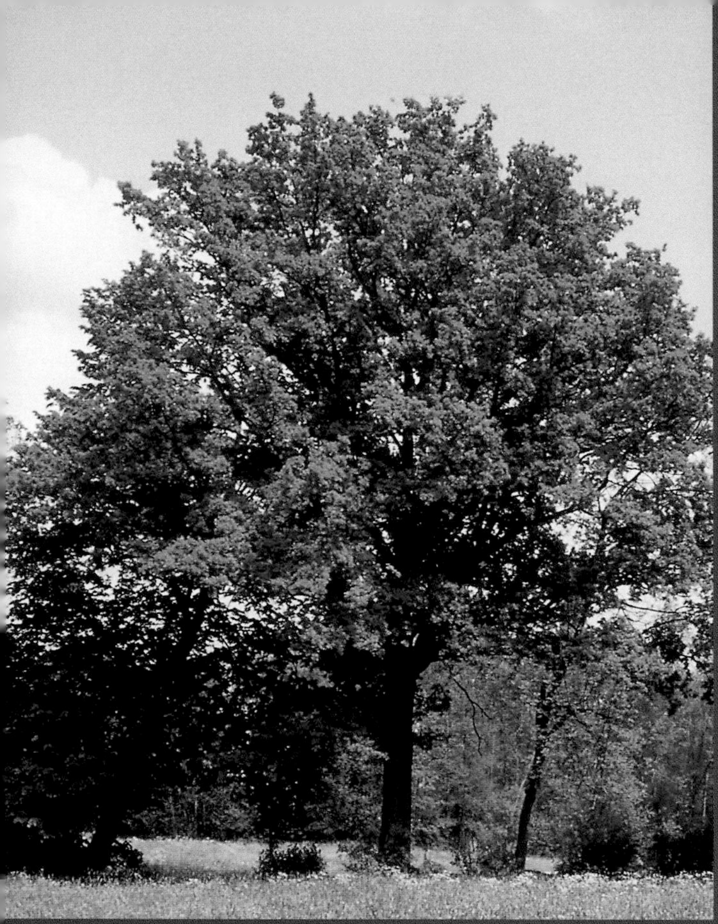

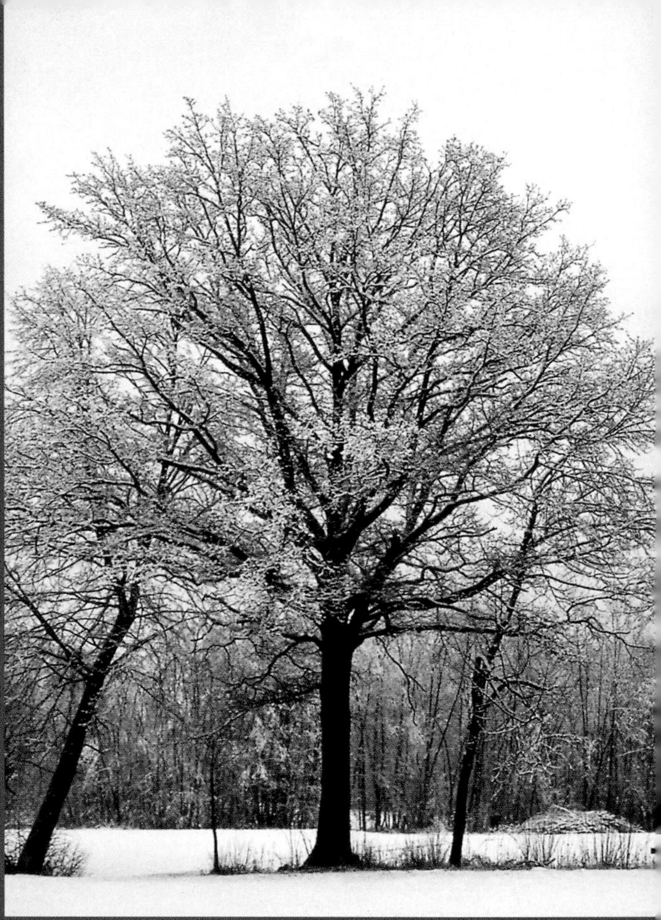

What has changed?